How to Match the Sky

How to Match the Sky

KENDALL HOEFT

RESOURCE *Publications* · Eugene, Oregon

HOW TO MATCH THE SKY

Resource Publications
An Imprint of Wipf and Stock Publishers
199 W. 8th Ave., Suite 3
Eugene, OR 97401

www.wipfandstock.com

PAPERBACK ISBN: 979-8-3852-5732-4
HARDCOVER ISBN: 979-8-3852-5733-1
EBOOK ISBN: 979-8-3852-5734-8

VERSION NUMBER 09/24/25

For every fish, especially those in reservoirs

For what is your life?

It is like a vapor that appears for a little while and then vanishes.

—James 4:14b

Contents

III. Water

IV. Plasma

Acknowledgments

I am grateful to the editors of the publications in which versions of the following poems first appeared:

Anti-Heroin Chic: "After Glass," "Songs of Summer," and "What We Don't Speak Of"

Artifact Nouveau: "Hidden Lady"

Bad Pony Magazine: "God Who Bloodies Knuckles"

Canyon Voices: "Southern Lady"

Driftwood Press: "How to Match the Sky"

Leveler: "Triassic Love"

Occulum: "Migration of a Hollow Swan"

Offline: "Of Sea and Sky," "Shock Me, Major Tom," and "When the Body Breaks"

Window (Patient Sounds): "Un-Realistic Fantasy for a Non-Functioning, Half-Asleep Flytrap"

ZiN Daily (Zvona i Nari): "Bathing my Father," "Southern Lady," and "Typology of Water"

"Bathing my Father" won the 2nd place prize in the 2020 Stephen A. DiBiase Poetry Contest.

"Poem I Didn't Write" was featured online in Tom Corrado's Poem-A-Day Project (2019).

"Migration of a Hollow Swan" was a finalist for the 2019 Stephen A. DiBiase Poetry Prize.

The poems "Of Sea and Sky," "Shock Me, Major Tom," and "When the Body Breaks" were showcased at AlbanyPoets.com.

I am thankful for the mentors, family and friends whose encouragement and expertise helped cultivate this collection.

I. Vapor

AROUND WE GO

After William Blake's *Elohim Creating Adam*

You still had that snake
                    wrapped up your thigh
    when your dust body
                    was breathed.
I laid on you
            like a dove, moved to make   you
more than flesh.

I left you awake,
longing upward,
the snake curled at your
feet.

TRIASSIC LOVE

I.
When you stretch your long green,
     I see
galaxies in your eyes—
black holes   extending
into a pre-creation sky.

Your neck moves smooth,
like a python in the Everglades—
maneuvering sawgrass marshes and pine flatwoods.

Your neck is a body.
Your neck is my heart
    and your heart,
       is good.

They say you are pre-historic,
which means you existed before.
Yet somehow, I remember dancing
your broad back,
leathered skin under naked toes.

Me, riding
you, pulling patches of soft
bamboo from the earth.

II.
I shoot up
        into crisp air,
as your head rises to meet sky.

I see a Microraptor,
its four wings, glossy and black.
I see an earth that knows only flesh and survival.
It doesn't understand our love—
how we survive.

III.
We glide underwater.
Between the lush
milky roots of water lilies,
Arandaspis appear—
their finless bodies
armored in knobby rows
like turtle shells
or crocodile feet.

When we emerge,
I nap with you
underneath me. You shimmy
around moody volcanos,
to keep me safe.

I hear you crunching on vegetation,
your wide eyes smiling to see mine.
We soak up the orange-red sky.

IV.
You do not speak of the battle,
your innocent neck gashed
deep and red.

I see
the ribbed scar.
I wrap
your neck.
I kiss
the tiny mountain range.
I swear
to always be with you, even in death.

WHAT WE DON'T SPEAK OF

Hushed tones, hushed tones.
We wouldn't want to stir the water,
or start a fight.

Keep positive, chin up.
The rest—
under the rug.

Or in the back room,
where father is in daughter's bed.

Hush.
We want to be happy.

Under quiet floorboards,
lie muted pieces—
in polite, hushed tones.

SHELTER

I.
Why did Jesus eat fish
        if He stands for non-violence?
        We pray for peace.
Christians don't give a shit about animals.

II.
I remember my first time
        seeing naked people,
                liberating.
I've been having flashbacks and crying uncontrollably.
        Pray for me?

III.
Unhappy,
in a ghost town mirage,
        I think
about having an affair
or seven.
I'm sick
of sleeping
with my   ghost.

IV.
Brother picks
     at sister's cockatiel
    until   *it pecks.*
He trips me
while I carry
     laundry.
He punches my arm
and hides
     under my bed,
     with a fire iron.

V.
Sisters, parents, brothers
    invite me
         to our living room
        during the crucifixion scene.
I try to leave.
They *pin me down*
    and laugh.
I scream.

They let me go.
I run into the neighborhood at night—
to find a tree,
to hide in.

HIDDEN LADY

My mama is from Missouri cornfields and ceaseless labor.
My mama is from grits, molasses and Baptist virtues.

My mama is from her mother,
edifice of self-martyrdom,
a woman who believes God loves you
as much as you've suffered,
who always sits in the hard chair,
who took her comb
while she was brushing her hair,
who misquoted the Bible,
vanity of vanities,
who taught her the wallflower half-life.

Now, when someone tells my Mama she is smart or charming,
she looks to the ground—
her weather-worn cheeks melting into a deep cinnamon.

I wonder
how long her hair would grow, if she knew
the glister of moon in her irises—
that she is the luminescent point
in a prolonged strangulation of sky.

POEM I DIDN'T WRITE

I. Eyes to See
Don't write a poem about me
and when, with walking stick in hand and your hand in the other,
I carried your brother on my back—
his dark curls collecting sunlight, as it broke
through tree tops and mixed with my breath
thick from climbing.

We threaded the mountain, making paths our own.
Flaky sheets of mica flashed translucent—
refracting beams of light like white-lipped oyster bellies.

Pyrite protruded from boulders. Its deceptive metallic luster
convinced children of faith. We believed
we could be gold miners. We believed
there were still nuggets in those Colorado hills.

II. Mountain Woman
You are a lumberjack.
You taught us to yell
timber while pushing dead trees.
You built a fort with a rope swing.
You carried a picture book that warned

which plants are poison.
You sang hymns. We nibbled wild raspberries and honeysuckle.
You showed us how to survive
on the mountain.

III. Stuck
Don't write a poem about me
and how in winter, when pipes froze,
we would drink
snow melted on the wood stove,
how blizzards kept our family together
inside, reading Proverbs
and *The Iliad* and practicing Latin
amo, amas, amat,
and pretending
we were *Little House on the Prairie*
as we collected
logs to burn.

IV. Detachment
Don't write a poem about me
and those slow evenings we snuggled
in your rocking chair.

I remember
the smell of leather and earth.
On your lap, I could tell you anything—
connected to you,
like I was when I floated inside you,
depending on you to provide
answers, until I began to answer my own questions.

I wonder if it felt like rebirth or a fracture—
like I was breaking off, out of you again.

I wonder now, if you can be happy with me,
apart from you.

ANATOMY OF CONNECTION

My lungs are bound to you.
My windpipe mimics your breath.
Even my stomach aches in a way it never has—
deep in my gastric folds, I hear intestines
squeezing out your name.

FRIENDSHIP LIKE BEES

I.
Our last day,
a bee landed between my toes.

I waited for her to fly,
but she only crawled
across the pad—
like she needed the soft of my foot's arch,
a shelter from the post-hurricane sea.

II.
I wonder why a bee stings if it kills her.
I wonder how long it'll take to recover.
I wonder if I'll always carry your torn abdomen inside me—
your memory, a beautiful irritation.

MURDER ON THE PORCH

I sprayed a wasp's nest—
got right in his territory
and pummeled him
with pesticides.

Now the corroded shell lays
on hard cement
withering—
a warning
to other stinging insects,
this house is not yours.

MIGRATION OF A HOLLOW SWAN

I.
I creep

> toward you—
> loud as a jaded Italian quartara,
> moonlit and brash.

In the celestial, I will die, and you will
forgive for decades shrouded in the dizziness of our magic.

II.
In spring, you are a grey house—
disinterested, thin as a sharp animal.
You never had a chance to live
voluptuous.
I can't remember the last
time
you pressed your barnacled sternum
to my chest   to confess—
a secret that's mostly clean.
You need a voice to adjust the ether
of incessant stinging,
hard roots and longing.

Love

brings not a few fractures.
Today I open my windows
to new guests awaiting spring.

II. Ice

AFTER GLASS

Hear the crackle of ice
on a hundred small lakes—

little lines jagging like hangnails
fragments of clear,
breaking off and jumping,
then breaking apart again.

We are held by compression.
Under the tension of our brittle surfaces
we are weak—
crystalline fabrications
incapable of keeping whole.

I leave shards on grey slate in my kitchen.

WHAT HOLDS HIM

His
cord
was
sizzled
black,
a rod
of
iron
up
his
back—
incense
to the
god of
the open
palm, She
scoliosis.
She,
steel
in
his
spine.

SOUTHERN LADY

Your mother is an edifice.
That fan, those jewels, these gloves
parasitized by that sweet potato whitefly
that is the South,
that is Alabama.

She could've grown like Grandma Lily's yellow verbena,
fragrant and wild
climbing holy to the sky.

Sometimes I think I see her blush.
I want to reach
ready to catch tears
before she powders powders powders powders.

When she returns from the ladies' room, I wonder what parts of
her are really here.
Her little white forearms, bricks in some Antebellum dam.

HOW TO MATCH THE SKY

The sky, like raw, ruddy bones over back-lit snow, speaks in tiny sparks—
scarlet pin pricks resurrecting
feathers over campfire.

The boy bathes in fear of her mouth.
Upon letting go, paper split his lips.

Now he hums to the wind, asking with a shield,
in this exhausted menagerie of voices—
bending like metal necks in fire, stretching to be seen.

BITTERSWEET

Come between
the twining—
      where
      life stoops,
little and mother-made.

Sway.
      Don't sway.
Sway.
      Can you do this
without stumbling?

Imagine unhooking her—
pulling vines,
root by root.

Would the body finally be
or would you come undone?

She needs rest, so she wraps
her furrowed orange and goes numb
making you still.

WILL YOU TAKE THIS WOMAN?

I.
Our eyes share little pleasures.
The core of a Sunday—
croissants in bed,
sequins, trumpets, tongues,
mirrors, tidal wave nights
you are all mine.

Surrender,
there is no such thing as sensibility.

II.
That mountain will kill
if you let it.
Let me show you
volcanoes that link us—
lessons harbored in solitude.
I take time to remember
how it felt to be un-brave.

III.
First, remember rain—
its smooth savor
hot and mute.

My body—
your forgotten Eucharist.

IV.
Let us take this moment.
Ingest my skin's pureness.
Croon for me
sweet and urgent
on knees, on your knees.
And I will trust your holy breath
to undo knots of flesh.
Break me free, for there is much of love
to learn.

HIGH AND DRY

Our love is in between—
my useless body
           stored like grain,
a winter that never comes.
I wait,
           hanging
pungent like lavender.
I break when touched.
I break to bits when you touch me.
How easily I come
apart   on   your   fingers.

HOW THE PEARL

I hold a fossil
which once lay
on the crushed-shell path
to your proposal.

You were calm
when you asked me
to sit on that Florida bench,
while you prepared
a picnic.

I meditated
on the river,
saw kids run
screaming after kites
and one solitary goose
floating.

My life winked.
I said a prayer.
I heard you speak my name.

WHAT THE CLOUDS SAY

Driving west across southern Florida,
I pass rest stops selling faux moccasins
and gator heads that once bobbed
like neon tourists floating.

Above this sweaty landscape, I see
shapes in clouds.
Creatures emerge from silver,
floating light in liquid droplets—
hydrogen and humidity,
dreams and desire.
I want
to ask if you see them too.

On the road, I think
how different we are—
how urgently I want the trash taken out,
how often I want to kiss you.

Do you see the bunny?
His translucent-grey ears
bright with sky,
his dark eyes dazzling—
like the Second Coming, sweet and terrifying.

BARRIER

Rosetta stone waits
under a wedding picture—
the one I look at to remember
how desire looks.

He doesn't know how to love
           with words
but sometimes,
he taps
           in code
when I need to feel
our rhythm.

Without a common tongue
we are two
wondering mouths:
    1.   a tourist
    2.   a language he's been meaning to learn.

UN-REALISTIC FANTASY FOR A NON-FUNCTIONING, HALF-ASLEEP FLYTRAP

I.

        Lure me,

        exotic plant.

        Tune

                my tongue

to   the key   of your   blue-green.

Infuse this air   viridian.

Release your love-drug, aphrodisiac.

II.

        I meditate on your smell of mint and musk

            drifting on the hairs

                of your inner surfaces—

          tickling trichomes   pubescent prickles

short straight soft

        hispid hairs.

You are triggered

        by my touch.

Seal me   in your succulent scent.   .

I am eager

        to feel your stomach

            churning my essence.

III.
Collapse on me.
Snap shut on me.
Dom me.
Pulverize my bones.
Squeeze me sapless.
Reduce me
   to a husk of chitin,
   a deserted exoskeleton,
   a surrendered shell.

R/REQUEST FOR BODY MODIFICATION

I.
as if I could
reach where you
accept this body
as yours
and move towards me
to make my body
your home.

II.
Can you make an impression
in my flesh? Melt skin with iron or pierce
layers with ink.

Make me yours,
into an image you can worship.

CITY OF LIGHTS

I. *Embrass*
I want
        to be kissed like the man is starving,
even if I break down like a robot sensing unprogrammed data.
What else is there to live for?

II. *Ingérer*
I want   to be   at ease   in my body.

III. *Oublier*
Where is the rope between safety and danger?
Let's swim in that waterfall
and fuck
the no trespassing signs.

Vodka
Coffee Liquor
Cream

I think his favorite
                he won't give me the   time of day
        is fading off to sleep
                when there's no
                        more to say.

SHOCK ME, MAJOR TOM

I am a hanging man
over a frozen lake.

I imagine plunging
your raw hypothermic water.
To be swallowed alive
must be the best way to ~~die~~ *live*

but, I must learn to be comfortable
with small deaths.
I try to paint
my dreams in a room
with a sleeping man, I want
to bring to life.
I need
to be more than the thing with a part that fits,
waiting for you to want me.

DREAMS IN MOURNING

I awake to the smell of lavender,
a steaming kettle,
two Persian cats in the window,
a husband scrolling Instagram.

I awake to the smell of coconut
two rare mahogany monkeys eating
newly picked pineapple and in the sunshine,
a chorus of swordfish.

I awake to the smell of cooking eggs,
an Iowa sunrise, honey in black coffee,
sweet and simple, hard work.
I can smell the blooming apple trees
swelling in fields of frosted clover.

FORGIVE US

I.
Stuck
       in the reservoir.
No sway,
water is a place
I am trapped.

Think of me, buckled upright.
I have made every preparation,
but this plane will not take off.

I still sense the other
buried
existing, in my body.
I never go there.

I don't allow my stomach
to vacuum into night air,
nothing that makes me sick or dizzy.

I'm not allowed to come
to the surface. So, I tighten
ready myself
for nothing.

Prepare to release
expectations,
but they claw me.
The bird inside me lives
holding on to the impossible crack
in her, like the little smile that broke lips.

II.
Dear boy, I ask my once lover,
am I invisible? I can't see myself.
Am I blind? I can't see you.

Things are slipping.
I spend so much time
without you,
I will arrive in concrete.
Eventually, all buildings turn to liquid.
I will be
pulled by my littlest wishbone
muscle flapping
bone snapping.
How lucky are you?

III.
They meet at end of day.
She talks about her life.
He falls asleep.
She misses going up with him
to gaze at the same stars.
She can barely remember
outstretched wings.

IV.
As I swim, I imagine
looking down on you
                remembering
your fingers holding mine.
Don't release my hands.
Don't stop
         my legs from shaking.
I'm good here. Examine my hubris.
Gaze down my lonely swan.
Can you see me drifting?

V.
Float in with me.
Let's wrap our bodies
like lotus roots,
eyes splayed and knees open.
Have we dipped too deep
to rise unmuddied?
Can we revive the dead between us?

VI.
Begin.
Hover   just below
bloom.
Kiss the experience of location.
Assert want onto me
like a stamp. Press me until
your energy is strained.

The mouths about us are still
jabbing, but we have stopped.
Slink into my feathers.

I continue to be both fish and reservoir
as I wait
for you
in my body, of water
to remember
what it feels like
to fly.

III. Water

TYPOLOGY (OF WATER)

We grow thirsty.
As city turns its back to water,
we question the waves—
searching for power
to resurrect our hope.

The shoreline carries promise
of suffocation, burial—
that inevitable sinking.

To rise in this paradigm, we must situate sea level,
                shift,
            complicate.

When transcendent, ask:
what is water?
Ask: is it prone to rising?

I want to talk about that liquid urban fabric—
a city of water conceived,
raised to respond to the rain.

BATHING MY FATHER

I. Sanctus
I wash your skin to the tunes of Zeppelin—
"Going to California," "In the Light Ocean,"
"Ten Years Gone."

You shift under water, searching for stillness.

Pupils flash like lures
under glassy flat corneas,
refractions of light—
waves under the surface.

I am a part of you;
a piece of me swam inside you.

How you must have cleansed me, too,
my tiny girl body
faultless and pure,
like a lamb without blemish or spot.

Tangled baby-hair
spread out weightless,
medusa in the water,
your little lion-head.

I must have stared,
floating in that deepest peace—
that is water,
that is Father.

When you spoke, *time is up*
did I whine, squirming like an eel?

Or jump up like first Baptism—
restored, euphoric, drunk on overflow,
my cup runneth over
                ready

for the warm towel and your voice,
this is my child, in whom I am well pleased.

II. Doxology
As you look up, I reach to give you what you need.
Holding your head, I soap up your white hair—
fluffy like an owl
puffy like Einstein.

When I rinse your scalp,
you make little purring sounds.

Careful not to let soap enter your eyes,
I pour slowly—
        let
        the
      warm
      water
        fall

over
your
wrinkled
widow's
peak.

I notice the lit pillar candle—
recurrent bits of bright
twitching in oscillating ripples.
Shivering feathers flutter,
this moment is divine. This moment is linear, eternal, good.

When I come back to the body,
we are one.

Gathering the soaked sponge, I begin again.

III. Benediction
I paint your parchment skin—
strokes up your canvas back,
down your long arms—
arms always wrapped around a favorite Fender.

Your hand over that fret board, fingertips vibrating
emotion expressible only through the blues.

This intimacy, it kept you up at night.

SONGS OF SUMMER

I. How He Found You
father and son

When the black wood bee found you,
he was roaring.

He roared when you ran through the sprinkler.
He roared when you laughed and cried.
He roared when you came in the front door, dripping.

When you tell me about the roaring black wood bee,
how he always found you, I want to put him in a jar of liquid.
I want to shake him, for you.

But when I tell you this, you only speak of the smell of honeysuckle,
Indian summers on Avenida de las Flores.

As you reminisce and laugh,
I recline, soothed and fading,
as we inhale the deepest breaths
of jasmine and geranium.

II. How You Found Him
As your mouth moves
specks of summer,
flecks of yellow light
effuse this Florida sunroom.

Childhood stories revive memories
of that suburban backyard utopia—
southern California in the '60s.

You caught bees,
shook them comatose,
buzzed bodies dulled
by the repetition of liquid in glass.

You pinned them to wood,
then waited;
wanting to watch death
overcome.

Did you know then he wouldn't come back?

III. Every Tarantula Hawk
You used to believe she was a child-created legend,
your boy-mind birthed fantasy.
Her long, black-blue body
bigger than a splayed hand.
Dark legs,
red wings—
hooked claws.

This creature would find the perfect hairy belly,
paralyze the large spider with a painful sting
then shave his abdomen clean and infest
her new nest with a spider-wasp egg.

You spent boyhood summers
watching the sky for these huge wasps,
looking for their spiders in the ground—
poking ice plants,
digging for life under blackness.

Two decades later, on that Colorado camping trip,
the origin of my arachnophobia,
you taught me to tease tarantulas from trap doors
with a relentless feather.

Now, even after hours,
you still poke into that large web
to see what you can awaken.

A THING HANDED DOWN

I. Under the Glaze
I like to think
the tobacco tinge
on this chipped white china
is you
breathing
into my new
apartment.

Sixteen years she served you
on these blue pastoral patterns—
your cigarettes warming desert nights,
collecting on her English dishes.

Neither of you had many nice things.
You lived in a trailer.
She cleaned houses,
you hung curtains
for forty years.

I can feel the warmth of water pouring
as she gently rinsed them clean.

II. Acid Resistant
There is a crackled stain,
no matter how much we wash,
that reminds of your stubbornness—
the fight to wake up
at 5am, and drink black coffee,
and research extra-terrestrials, and go to drag races,
and feel what you could, and kiss my Grandma,
and drink until your eyes rocked like black holes
and your body fell to earth in envelopes
and sweet Jesus took your boy-spirit home.

And still, I love your muck
and cherish any musk I can recall
as though you are blowing
into my dining room
and I am hugging your rock-hard belly,
still wanting you to be proud.

III. Colors Permanent
You never meant to fuck him up.
Your boy was sunshine and hope—
an impossible star
birthed in a galaxy of unknown darkness.
Though you couldn't say it
you were prouder of him
than anything you'd ever dreamed of.

WE ASK THE LIAR

if he is lying
because we hope
to see him
    waking
        in the sun
opening a window
        releasing
stagnant air
      breathing
    allowing light
        to move in him again.

We want him
    to bind our heart
with sentences,   we can trust
honest words.

But he is always haunted
by the terrible music
of a life unlived—
a father's swan song,
the bottle,
old mistakes.

FATHER KALEIDOSCOPE: AN EXAMINATION OF BIPOLARIZED LIGHT

I.

You promised once
you'd let me see, so I looked
hopeful, as one does

   into a kaleidoscope.

II.

You are an ever-changing pattern.
Which slivers are you?
Which are refractions?

The large pieces
don't transmit much light.
They are hard to see
but still
they tumble
when the cell is rotated—
they jumble with motion
into shapes—
fragments haphazard
   and perfect. Your light
   and dark

emerge in patterns—
mirrored constructions of you.

III.
You've always been a black and white boy—
waiting with mother at the laundry mat
and on the way home, dropping
fresh clothes off the back of your radio flyer
like confused star clusters in an asphalt nebula.

You want to be pure,
so you live segmented,
neglecting your shadow.

IV.
You are impossible for me
to put together
but still wish I could
reflect your loose parts,
so you could observe the beautiful form
of your symmetrical mosaic motif.

V.
You are every good and bright thing
that learned to hide in the cutting winter,
every red-winged sparrow with a song,
every cocoon-cracking spirit longing to break free.

IV. Plasma

GOD WHO BLOODIES KNUCKLES

He never saw Mother Superior before
a girl tripped playing red rover, and he was sent—
ascending stairs, like rosary beads,
hesitating, praying, climbing.

Inside her office, a thick mahogany desk—
small deities sprawled like crocuses on a casket.
She unleashed the crucifix from her neck
to strike his outstretched hands.

He doesn't go by Michael anymore.
I'm not an angel. I'm a man, he says.

I leave him on his park bench
watching iguanas on river rocks—
their thin-skinned bodies soaking in light.

PAS DE DEUX

After Naomi Shihab Nye's "Fresh"

to move cleanly
into new light—
    resurrection,
        black earth
        turned over
again
    my shadow says
    he wants
to protect   me
but he is not real
only I AM
here
in heavy flesh,
making space
for bloom.

BLOOM CACTUS BLOOM

What kind of creature bites and sucks the last flower
and slinks around the rough, green spine to snap its yellow-cream bloom?

I suppose the lizard is thirsty—
obsessive, with an irreverent shake,
continuing to exist, to tremble
to slink, if necessary,
despite the heat
shattering rocks
fragments lifted
by dust storms
in circles
in circles
containing nothing
sand grains striking
depleted desert
empty and unkind.

WHEN THE BODY BREAKS

I.
Somebody asks
how we count
in this world,
but I can't recall.

In the beginning
we imagined our poems
digging,
found strange things from other places
and waved the very best of them.

We learned early
how to smear our tongues
on every weeping morsel,

how artist needs body,
how we must taste the food we eat.

II.
We listen high
to the heavy hum of Monday.

Our bodies dropped low or doped up—
cough-syrupped and crazy-glued.

Our eyes fixed
on the same incapacitated star—
her moon-tides always creeping,
wherever you go.

III.
Ah dear Jesus, we wait
for any new light.

I have been making this effort, Lord.

Despite myself, I believe
there is a very real future
nothing like what I see.

ARABESQUE

I am no geometric figure—
cannot move
in a line. Inside my body:
intertwining foliage
confused tendrils
pulsating waves
writhing clusterfucks.

I am always supported
by one leg,
while the other extends
backward.

SWALLOWING

When I sit drinking
I am not thinking
of the fast or fallen—
fragments of light
free-styling through a lucid sky.

I am not thinking
of where I should be
or how I spent the last five hours
on this leather spot.
Only: permission, surrender.

Sometimes nothing feels better.
Empty a glass or four of this
Cabernet—
little red rock star,
ready and reeling to be
the ruffian in my belly
loosening me up
as my wild hair shakes
power chords of release.

MOOD SWING IN B MINOR

You're not to believe a word of it, even if it's true.
—Hazel Gaynor, The Cottingley Secret

Feel the music;
    don't complicate the steps.
Only take
                    what lights your bones
the rest—
sawdust, chaff in wind, grinds
      at the bottom. You are heavy
      hoisting sacks into your mind.
      None of your business
none of your business. But I am kept
      shaking   long into night
                  after they are asleep
and a little drool is sticking his soft lips.

I look over and see he's satisfied
      then growl—roaming in dark complexities
stomach prickling, like I've had too many
or not eaten or someone cheated
    took advantage of my optimism   or
didn't see me. And I'm really not in bed

but standing   in reflective silver
maybe bodiless
shivering
naked and uncertain of the beauty.

OF SEA AND SKY

Sometimes she did not know what she feared, what she desired:
whether she feared or desired what had been or what would be,
and precisely what she desired, she did not know.

—LEO TOLSTOY, ANNA KARENINA

I.
I've never seen a living oyster
though I have eaten them
and worn pearls around my neck.

II.
Beyond the no trespassing sign,
we found a waterfall.
Splashing, I grasped for something I'm not sure exists—
something I might always attempt to find and hold.

III.
Why don't eagles band together?
I know they aren't cogs,
geese in symmetry,
but still it is easier
to get a bunch of people dancing
when you begin with two.

IV.
I met a woman who is carefree, so I am
learning to be more open.
I'm not sure friendship is possible,
but I am attempting to find
harmonies
between absence
and presence.

V.
Shaken, I settle into new shapes
bright and strange—
like a kaleidoscope
or a game of musical chairs played by
luminescent fish on the ocean floor.

VI.
I play the idea of reinvention
in my record player.
I wonder if transformation is possible
or if we are just clams with one unchanging pearl inside us.